# SOME OF THAT
# *"Bea" Wisdom*

By

# DIANNE GRIGGS

Dedicated to My Mother, Beatrice Robertson

*February 16, 1921–March 15, 1983*

*Child, if you don't stay out those stores, you won't have
bloomers to put on your hind parts.* –Beatrice Robertson

# Dedicated to My Mother,

## *Beatrice Robertson*

### *February 16, 1921–March 15, 1983*

# Foreword

*"When wisdom enters into your heart, and knowledge is pleasant unto your soul;*

*Discretion to shall preserve you, understanding will keep you to deliver you from the way of evil...."*

*Proverbs 2: 10-12a NKJV*

Wisdom is not understood always when it is first heard, especially when one is a child or "coming of age" as a teenager! It is understood or received, even less, when the words are emanating from the lips of a parent and are a part of a list of instructions, directions or idioms meant to keep one in line. However, the power of wisdom is in its similarity to a seed. It starts out very inconspicuously, like any group of words. However, the "life" that is hidden in these words is rooted in a truth that transcends time, location and generation. Its results are often the fragrant flowers and sturdy oak trees that give peace and strength along our journeys through life.

In her book, **Some of That Bea Wisdom**, Pastor Dianne Griggs take the time to show us the results of the seeds of the wisdom planted by her mother, lovingly called Bea, over the years as she grew up in a loving family being one of 15 children, through losing her firstborn son, being twice widowed and eventually, becoming a pastor of a church. This is not a story of the trials and tribulations that one might experience going through. On the contrary, it is a compilation of idioms, the seeds of wisdom that her mother sowed into her life along the way! As Pastor Dianne shows the details of the seeds, we begin to see how interesting life can be, if the seeds are received in the good soil of our spirits!

What was exciting for me was that as Pastor Dianne writes, I felt something familiar about her mother! As I read each of the sections, I could hear the sweet, but serious voice of my own mother. Even though she transitioned into her eternal home in 2000, I could sense her voice telling me some of the same things... some of which I did and some of what I wish I had done!! (oops---must take a tear break!!!) That "Bea Wisdom" went even further. It even reminded me about the seeds of wisdom that were sown into my life not only by my biological mother, but all of the "mothers" (and fathers) that God had sent to me during my life!

This is a wonderful book for those who just want to remember the blessings that have been given to them from others. It is for those who have received the seeds of wisdom and can "take time to smell the flowers" or to "sit in the shade of a tall oak tree". It is a source of inspiration for everyone. But it is especially inspiring for those whose mothers have transitioned to their Heavenly home.

So, as you read this, don't be surprised if you sense the presence in your spirit of someone whose voice you haven't heard in a long time. Moreover, don't be surprised if you hear yourself telling the same things to your children.

Pastor Dianne has done a great job in capturing just a few of the many great seeds of wisdom that her mother sowed into her. And, if by any chance you've never heard of them, then this will be a chance for you to experience "Some of That Bea Wisdom".

Thank you, Mother Bea for the seeds of wisdom that you gave your daughter, Pastor Dianne. You also gave them to us! To God be the Glory!

*"It's a Wisdom Thing....You Must Understand!!!"*


Rev. Debyii L. Sababu-Thomas, Ph.D.

June 2016

# Table of Contents

# Introduction

*Child, if you don't stay out those stores, you won't have bloomers to put on your hind parts.* –Beatrice Robertson

Listen, my son, to your father's instruction
and do not forsake your mother's teaching.
They are a garland to grace your head
and a chain to adorn your neck. *Proverbs 1:8-9 (NIV)*

The scripture above is one of the proverbs of Solomon, the son of David, King of Israel. During Solomon's time, both parents participated in the education of their children. As a result, children had the benefit of both the paternal and maternal aspect of situations and circumstances. This passage emphasizes that we should listen and receive wisdom, that wisdom is beautiful and valuable. To have it is like a crown on one's head, or it is like a gold chain around the neck. Another proverb states, "Wisdom is supreme; therefore get wisdom. Though it cost all you have, get understanding" (Proverbs 4:7, NIV). To obtain wisdom, we must be willing to listen to sound advice, and we need discipline. We cannot become wise overnight. But if we obtain wisdom, it will benefit us more than fame, money, or any other material thing. Nothing is greater than wisdom. If we have wisdom, we can get money; but without wisdom, no amount of money will last very long (Proverbs 17:16). Wisdom and education are not the same thing.

It has been said that the difference between education and wisdom is in how the mind is used. Education focuses on formal and informal problem-solving methods using logical thinking along with enhanced knowledge to invent, create, and design solutions to problems. Wisdom, however, comes from collecting experiences and recombining those experiences in intuitive rather than formal ways to solve problems. Education sometimes comes with a very high price tag, but wisdom is free. We can ask God for wisdom about any specific situation or circumstance in life, and he will GIVE it to us—not sell it, not lend it, but give it to us freely. My mother knew that, and unbeknownst to me, she tapped into that unending Source.

I am one of 15 children born to my late parents, Waddell and Beatrice Robertson. My mom and dad were married on Christmas Eve in the year 1945. When my dad died, they had been married 31 years. My mother was born on February 16, 1921 and was raised in Washington, DC, the city of her birth. She departed this earthly life on March 15, 1983 after living just 62 brief years. She attended public schools in the District of Columbia: Anthony Bowen Elementary, Randall Junior High, and Cardoza Senior High schools. She was a graduate of the Cortez Peters Business College. During her career with the Federal Government, she was employed at the Bureau of the Census and the Pentagon. She attended the Temple Church of God in Christ (COGIC) located in Northwest DC during most of her early years and later was a member of Emmanuel COGIC, Southeast DC.

Bea worked briefly outside of the home, but her children were born in such quick succession that going out of the home to work became impractical. First came Clarice, followed closely by my brothers Waddell, Jr. (now Sultan Muhammed) and Chester Lee. (For some reason that has always escaped me, Chester was the only one of us who was given a middle name.) My sisters, twins Joyce and Gloria, and I followed. The six of us were born within 2 years of each other. My other siblings—brothers Marvin and Martin (twins), Michael, Gary, and Darrell; and sisters, Billie, Donna, Gail, and sadly the unnamed, unknown, and still missed stillborn baby—all followed closely. The two sets of twins that my mother bore, coupled with the fact her brother (my only maternal uncle) also had a set of twins, made me very fearful of becoming pregnant with twins. At that time, I could not imagine having more than one child! Being raised with so many siblings left me a bit shell-shocked, and quite frankly, not desirous of having any children at all. Fortunately, that feeling changed for me.

Bea rarely spoke about my deceased siblings who both died in infancy—my brother Marvin's twin, Martin, and my little sister Gail. On the rare occasions when she did talk about them, she would become reticent, her tone somber, and her comments very brief. However, once she did tell me that baby Martin had been very precocious. She said that at a very early age he would roll himself over and attempt to sit up in his bassinet. She was so proud of him and the things he could do. She thought that she might have taken him outside too much as an infant. I just hoped that she did not in some way blame herself for what seemed to have been his untimely passing.

I do not recall her ever talking about my baby sister Gail. I can only imagine what my mother must have gone through, what she had to endure. With other small children to care for, there was no time to fully grieve. That was a luxury that she could not afford. We were too young to give her sympathy. She could not share her feelings with us, and my dad was always working. Sometimes I think about my deceased siblings and the brevity of their lives. I find myself wishing that I had probed a little to get more details about their lives and deaths. I do not know where they died, what they died of, or where they are buried (if they were buried). I have no recollection of a funeral or any kind of service. You must understand, I grew up during the time when many adults believed that children should be seen and not heard, and such matters were considered "grown folks' business."

Bea worked outside the home for only a brief time. Her working career ended, she told me, on the day she came home and learned from the babysitter that I had fallen into the commode! She was fiercely protective of her children. She could not understand how something like that could have happened if the babysitter had been doing her job. So she decided right then to stay home and take care of us herself. She said that if she was going to pay a sitter who was not going to give us her full attention, she might as well stay home with us and pay herself. What a commitment! What wisdom!

For most of my mother's early years, she attended the Temple Church of God in Christ in Washington, DC, under the leadership of the late Bishop Samuel Kelsey. Yes, COGIC, where the motto was "You can't join it. You have to be born in it." That was the Holiness faith, and Bea was holy to the bone! The only thing I could do as a teenager that she would bless was attend church! If I asked her to go to a friend's house or to some evening activity, her response was always the same: Go get yourself ready for school the next day (if it was a weekday) or for church (if it was the weekend). Her view was that if you took the time you needed to properly prepare for the next day, you did not have time to do anything else, especially on a school night. Young people become bored very easily. If I or other siblings said we were bored, she'd say, "read a book." If we asked to visit a friend to play or to have friends visit us at our house, her response was, "You have enough brothers and sisters to do anything you need to do." Well, there certainly was no disputing that! Bea also told us that the less time you spent with some people, the better off you would be. Her words were "association breeds assimilation." She did not want us to copy the behaviors of others who may not have been raised with her Christian values.

In today's vernacular, Bea would be called a stay-at-home mom. Back in the day, she was called a housewife. She was as smart as a whip, witty, and unflappable.

People enjoyed talking to her because she was a great conversationalist. She could talk about anything, and she could be depended upon to not repeat things that were shared with her in confidence. Bea never divulged to me anything shared with her by my other siblings. In fact, it was only after her transition that I heard about many things that she had done for certain family members. I learned about it from them, not Bea. She never talked to one of her children about another one. Bea was the rock of the family. Although she was not the eldest, everyone leaned her. If there was a dispute within the family, all of the involved persons would call my mother to tell her their side of the story. She was a good listener. She would let each one tell his or her side of the story and would offer only an occasional comment. She never took sides; she was only on the side of right. If one of us tried to criticize another sibling, Bea would not hear of it. She would quip, "Get out of my face; that's the pot calling the kettle black." It was from my mother that I learned not to take sides but to be on the side of right.

Bea had flawless diction and great writing ability. Her beautiful, delicate penmanship were in sharp contrast to the strong discipline those hands dished out when needed. Nowadays, people do not believe in spanking their children, but Bea believed in and took literally the expression, "spare the rod, spoil the child." But she did not always spank us. She said that if she gave us the spanking that we really needed, it would kill us, and she did not want to kill her children. So, sometimes she would hit us with that wisdom whip that made you feel so bad you thought you had been hit but she had not laid a hand on you! I know that she was a praying woman because some of the things we did had to drive her up the wall. But she was always patient and soft spoken, even when disciplining us.

I think it was music that helped her deal with so many of us. She would sit at the piano in our dining room and play. The melodies would drift throughout the house and somehow bring a sense of calm. Music not only has charms to soothe a savage beast; it can also quiet a house full of hyped-up children. Looking back, I believe that my mother knew that. I believe that oftentimes when Bea was tickling the ivory and singing, she was doing it to calm herself and to quiet us. She also played piano for her church, where she was a devoted member.

My father, on the other hand, rarely attended church. He also was not much of a talker, but like the character in a once-popular EF Hutton commercial, "when he spoke, everybody listened". I have no recollection of him ever reading the Bible, but he seemed to subscribe to the passage in Ecclesiastes that admonishes us to let our words be few. He was a hard worker, the breadwinner of the family, a real workaholic. However, he was always there for my mother. He took her everywhere she went, picked her up, and brought her home. She would stand waiting at the gate in the backyard. My father would pull the vehicle up to the gate, put my mother in, and off they would go. When they returned, he would drive up to the backyard gate so that my mother could get out of the car. She would go into the house through the screened in porch that opened into our big, sunlit country kitchen, and then sit down. Whatever was in the car, we kids brought it in. If it was groceries, we put them away at Bea's direction. I liked that part because I got to see exactly what we had and would, unbeknownst to my mother, schedule a late-night sneak to clandestinely retrieve a cookie or some other treat I had spied earlier. Lord, forgive me!

My mother was a lovely big-boned woman, who enjoyed beautiful things, a lot of which she did without so that her children could have the things they needed. I often would say to her, jokingly of course, that she had too many children and that she should have stopped with me. You can probably guess how well that went over. Bea loved clothes and really knew how to put her clothes together. She did not care much for shopping in department stores but rather ordered everything from a catalog. I can recall helping her get dressed. She was fastidious in her dress and took ample time to lay out every piece of clothing, including matching shoes and handbag, before she went to bathe. Once she came out of the bathroom, the process would begin—Vaseline for her feet, lotion for her body and baby powder all over. I loved to watch her get dressed. Sometimes, she would ask for my help in fastening her stockings to her garters. I remember seeing baby powder cascading down like new fallen snow from her body onto the hardwood floors and sometimes on my head. After she was completely dressed, I would follow her as she went down the stairs, looking good and smelling even better, and Diddy (not P Diddy, but our affectionate name for our father), stood outside with the "coach" waiting.

For the most part, Diddy was pretty reserved. When he came home from work, he deposited his metal lunch box on the table. Shortly thereafter, the leftovers in that lunchbox were hotly contested among us. (Ummm, I can smell them now, warm from being either in the truck Diddy drove for the city or sitting somewhere in the sun). My father got up before dawn and was usually out of the door and on his way to work while we were still dreaming. But I was the fortunate one who would sometimes wake up early and make my way sleepily down the wooden staircase which spilled into what we called the "front room," back into the kitchen where Diddy was.

My earliest recollection of Diddy is of him preparing his own breakfast and packing his own lunch. Diddy was from North Carolina and did not always prepare the traditional DC breakfast—cereal and milk or eggs, bacon, and toast. Oh, no! I would sit with my feet swinging at the table and salivate at the aroma of the fat back as Diddy fried it. I could hardly contain myself as he made dough and knuckled it down into hot oil in my mother's heavy, black, cast iron skillet. It smelled so good. He let it get brown on one side; then, he would flip it over. Sometimes he would do a trick for me and not use the pancake turner but throw the thick, round bread (called hoecake) high in the air and catch it with the pan and let it finish cooking. After he finished cooking the hoecake, Diddy would plop a healthy scoop of real butter on top of it. Then, he would go to the cabinet and pull out that big blue can of molasses, scoop out that thick, dark, rich, sweet liquid and pour it on that hot hoecake. The butter and the molasses would soften and run down the hot bread, down around the edge of the plate. Oh my! I can almost taste it now! That was some good eating. Diddy would pick up a forkful, eat a bite, then pass me a bite. I felt so privileged and special, eating with my dad while the others slept. I could hardly wait for my siblings to wake up. Before they could wipe the Sand Man from their eyes, the news flash was on my lips, and I would proudly, sometimes tauntingly say, "I had breakfast with Diddy." Everybody knew what that meant. I stood in a class by myself. I had an advantage they did not share—

time alone with our father, and a sizzling hot, home-cooked breakfast.

For his lunch, Diddy would sometimes make another hoecake, wrap it up with some fatback, and put a beverage in his tall, metal thermos. In the evening, some of my siblings and I waited anxiously for Diddy to come home. Yes, we wanted to see him but we also wanted to get our hands on his lunch box to get his leftovers.

Looking back now, it seems just crazy! When the container was opened, in my child's mind, it seemed that the leftovers smelled like work, if that was possible. However, that did not matter, nor what was in it; all eyes were on that lunch box when he got home, and may the best man win! Just imagine if you will, five or six children (sometimes more), scrambling across the kitchen floor, pushing and shoving, screaming to the top of their lungs "I've got it!" But there was only one lunch box and its contents were few. Needless to say, there were many sore losers. My parents were so patient. I do not remember them ever scolding us for acting so nutty! They probably found it rather amusing.

Before he went upstairs to change his clothes for dinner, Diddy would sit at the kitchen table with my mother and she would discuss the events of the day with him. Sometimes, the conversation was in hushed but clearly heard or understood tones. At other times, Bea and Diddy would have a lively exchange and would chuckle here and there. Oh, but when the conversation became low and muffled, if any of us who were within earshot had misbehaved that day, fear would strike our hearts. Surely, Bea was telling Diddy on us! Yes, she was the disciplinarian in the family, of necessity because she was the one who was most often with us. Bea exacted discipline on the spot! You got it where you did it. She wanted there to be no doubt what the punishment was for. You had no time to forget. However, wisely, she did not exclude my father from this role either. She never prevented him from exercising his role as head of the household and leader of his family. Even after she had disciplined us, she would let him know what we had done and what she did about it. If it was warranted (and trust me, sometimes it was), my father would seek out the disobedient child and reinforce what my mother had said and done.

Before I go any further (I probably have already gone on too long), let me explain why we called our mother "Bea." Well, first of all, that was her name! I got you there, didn't I? But honestly, it was because for a long time during our early childhood years, my grandmother shared our home with us. My mother was really close to her mom—just as she and I were. They talked throughout the day. My mother always called my grandmother "Momma," and my grandmother called my mother "Bea." Like most children, we simply repeated what we constantly heard. We called our grandmother Momma and my mother Bea. Neither one of them ever corrected us or indicated that anything was wrong or told us to do anything other than that. So, for as far back as I can recall, and to this very day, my mother has been Bea.

To me, Bea, was the wisest women on God's green earth. Although she did not work outside of the home and, as far as I could tell during my younger years, she went no further than to church and the grocery store. Still, Bea seemed to know everything. Before we left for school or work, she gave us the traffic and weather reports. If there was something untoward taking place or predicted anywhere along our travel route, she made us aware of it. And, if anything transpired in and around the neighborhood that could be harmful to us, she was known for sending our brothers to bring us home from wherever we might be, oftentimes kicking and screaming! But they had their orders and bring us home they did! They enjoyed hearing us scream "put me down", as we resisted what seemed to us to be brute force, which had been sanctioned by our mother to get us out of harm's way. Bea was an avid reader and loved talk-show radio and TV broadcasts. She read the newspaper daily, as well as other magazines and periodicals. She was always abreast of what was going on.

My mother made her transition to be with the Lord on my only son's birthday. That is a day that I hate to remember but one that is forever etched in my memory. It was Tuesday, March 15, 1983. Ashanté had just turned 8 years young. The US president was Ronald Reagan (Republican). In that special week of March, people in US were listening to "Billie Jean" by Michael Jackson. *The Meaning of Life*, directed by Terry Jones, was one of the most viewed movies released in 1983. But the meaning of my life was forever changed because gone was the one who not only gave me life but also gave my life the most meaning!

That Tuesday started no differently than most. I got up, prepared for work, and dropped Ashanté at my mother's house. Bea took care of him and a few of her other grandchildren while we parents worked. Nothing out of the ordinary transpired during the workday, nothing that would alert me to or prepare me for the awful occurrence to come later. I left work and made the usual 25–30-minute trip to my mother's house to collect my baby boy. All was well. We did our usual. Bea was sitting in her big, comfortable armchair, which was upholstered in her favorite color, and now mine—red. The chair was located near the front door. That's where she most often sat at that time of day—probably watching the door, hoping and praying that we would hurry up and come collect our children whom she had been lovingly taking care of all day and was by now tired of and ready to be relieved of them. I came in, greeted her, and flopped down in another chair opposite her, as though I had been the one tending four or five little ones all day. We talked, and we talked, and we talked. This was our way. It seemed that no matter how often we saw each other, and we saw each other every day, we still had something to talk about. Then when I got home, I would call back, and we would talk some more. I just loved talking to my mother. I phoned her so much that my youngest sister and cousins who lived with my mother, would often say when I called, "Didn't you just leave here? Didn't you just speak to Bea?" My response would be, "Just put my mother on the phone," and they did. That Tuesday, March 15, 1983 was no different, except we had a little more to talk about. After all, it was my son Ashante's birthday, and I was planning a big birthday party for him that weekend. It was going to be held at my mother's house. It was a tradition. I had all of his birthday parties there. These were always elaborate, themed parties and well attended by my family and friends. So, we talked about that and a variety of other things. Then, I packed up Ashanté and went home.

After I got home and got settled, I called back and spoke to my mother, as usual. Later that evening, my phone rang and the call was coming from my mother's house. I was not the one who initiated the call this time. It was my baby sister, and she was speaking rapidly, in an urgent tone. She was very upset. She said I needed to come back to the house because Bea was sick. She had already called for an ambulance. Her words cut me like a knife. I do not remember what I did or the sequence in which I did it. I can only tell you that it seemed that instantly I was back at my mother's house. When I arrived on the scene and saw the emergency vehicle, my heart sank, and I knew inexplicably that my mother was gone. Nevertheless, I entered the house and with trepidation mounted the familiar but now daunting staircase.

Once at the top, I made the right turn a few feet into my mother's bedroom where paramedics were administering life-giving aid in an attempt to revive her. All of their efforts were useless. Bea was already no more. They put my mother's lifeless body in the ambulance and transported her to DC General Hospital, where she was pronounced dead. I drove my car to the hospital and arrived shortly after. When I heard that final declaration, I could not breathe. It seemed that my heart stopped beating and every bit of air had been sucked out of the room. "Oh, no," I screamed! Knowing what I already knew but was unwilling to accept. My precious Bea, my role model, my confidante and biggest fan, my mother, was gone. My sister said that in the minutes before her passing, Bea was sitting in her room on the side of her bed saying, "Lord, your will be done" and "God is in control." Bea was wise in life and wise in death.

When Bea transitioned from this life to life eternal, she was a member of Emmanuel Church of God in Christ (COGIC), also located in Washington, DC. She gave her life to Christ at an early age and lived for Him every day. The Bible says that the fear of the Lord is the beginning of wisdom. Well, Bea surely did fear God and did her best to please Him. Yes, she was truly a wise woman. I can recall her getting my sister and brothers and me together and teaching us Bible verses and singing gospel songs while she accompanied us on the piano. She taught us to love God, one another, and ourselves.

I must admit that there were many times when I discussed matters with my mother that I certainly was not always seeking wisdom. I just wanted things to work out—mostly the way I wanted them to work out. She always had something to say that helped on some level, even if it was not what I wanted to hear. She gave me practical advice about boys when I was a girl and about men when I grew up. She also told me about finances, relationships, and life in general. She imparted so much wisdom in me before I knew God or had a relationship with Him. In hindsight, I am so grateful to God for the time we had together, whether cooking for big, family dinners or doing her hair. I always treasured our time together. I was a Bea addict! Everybody knew how much I loved my mother. After I married and left home, our relationship intensified. Whenever I went out and found myself anywhere in the vicinity of her house, I stopped by to see her, and I loved buying things for her.

I bought clothes, shoes, trinkets and what she referred to as "what nots"—clowns and elephants, which she collected. Sometimes, I would take a day off from work, go to the store and get her favorite foods, cook, and we would eat and talk. Just recounting those times here, in these pages, causes my heart to swell with love and gratitude for her. She shared so much with me, and I have shared it with people I have met. Although Bea is gone from my physical sight, she is ever present in my heart. The things she said to me still resonate today.

Even when I was a young girl, people sought me out for answers to various dilemmas in their life. I did not really understand why. I would simply tell them what Bea had told me, and it would work for them. As I grew older and began developing a relationship with God and studying His word, I discovered that the counsel that my mother had given me was scripturally based. However, when talking to me, she rarely prefaced her words with "the Bible says." She knew what was written in Isaiah 55:11—"so is my word that goes out from my mouth: It will not return to me empty, but will accomplish what I desire and achieve the purpose for which I sent it." She knew that if she kept saying "the Bible says," we would probably have ignored her. Bea knew that all she had to do was speak the word, and God would do the rest! She was wise enough to know that because she was feeding us the word of God, it could not fail. Because of Bea, people who are in my sphere of influence, often unknowingly are the benefactors of the wisdom my mother shared with me.

I am forever grateful to God for giving me Bea as my mother. Because of her godly influence, the life she lived, and the wisdom she imparted, I have been able to navigate the waters of life; deal with difficulties, perplexities, and uncertainties; and still have joy. I only wish that my daughter Samantha had known her. Samantha was born October 7, 1988, more than 2 decades after my mother's transition. Bea would have just loved her. In some ways, she is just like her grandmother. Thank God for DNA.

When Bea departed this life, she left me a magnanimous treasure, one worth more than money. She left me wisdom! And what she gave me, I added to it, and I do not intend to stop. I have found out that wisdom really is the principal thing. So, I'm going to share some of the wisdom morsels Bea shared with me that have blessed my life. You will not find many dates in the material shared because this is not a chronology. The "when" is unimportant because wisdom is timeless. It was good enough for her then and it is good enough for me now. I have no doubt that it will be good enough for you, too.

That "Bea Wisdom"

# On Marriage

*"If you can take it, you can make it."*

I would never flat out tell my mother that anything was going wrong. But she had something that I did not become familiar with until many years later, that is, the gift of discernment. She could always tell without me saying one word that something was up! No matter how I tried to hide it or make her believe the call was about something other than what it was, Bea knew. Sometimes, I would just say hello, and she would say simply, "trouble in paradise?" Well, I must admit, sometimes it had to do with the hour that I called. I can recall one time in particular when I was in my early 30s. I had been married for a few years to a wonderful man.

Looking back, I can see that I was really immature; and, surprisingly, although I came from a very large family, I was also spoiled. I wanted to have my way, and when I did not get it, I would sulk and pout until I did. But it was all my husband's fault (of course)! I was truly blessed. He was a devoted husband and father and also a loving son. He dearly loved and cared for his mother. Now let me take time right here to pass on Some of That Bea Wisdom. Draw in close now because this is very, very important. Bea told me, "Watch to see how a man treats his mother. You will not get better than that." I can certainly say that was true in my case, and I have found it to be true in the lives of friends. Now back to my story.

My husband, God rest his beautiful soul, was 7 years my senior and a divorcé with three children. My wise mother had counseled against marrying him, not because he was not a good person, but because she said, "Baby, that's a nice boy but he's not the boy for you. Child, that boy is tired. You need somebody starting out like you're starting." Wow, the wisdom those words contained. Did I listen? No, of course not. I had selective hearing. I only heard what I wanted to hear—that he was nice, and she liked him. However, she was right. He was a wonderful husband and a great father but he had been through a lot, and he was tired. I, on the other hand, was vibrant and inquisitive. I had lived a very sheltered life, and everything was new and exciting to me. I soon became bored, so bored in fact that I told my mother I did not want to be married any more. Here she comes with that Bea Wisdom.

My mother said, "Child, if you weren't going to have another man, I would tell you to go ahead and leave. But since I know you're going to have someone else, you need to settle yourself down. You have a good husband, and those things that you're talking about are small and won't matter much after a while." According to Bea, any marriage that has lasted for any length of time has lasted because the people involved decided to "take" something. They understood that everything could not be just the way they wanted it. "If you can take it, you can make it." She was absolutely right.

Many marriages fail because the parties involved, either one or the other, do not want to take anything. There are, of course, certain things that people should not stand for, such as physical abuse or a spouse whose modus operandi is adultery (different from a lapse in judgment, resulting in a mistake that is not constantly repeated). If people would learn how to take something, to value commitment, to esteem others above themselves, to allow someone else to be right and not record every wrong done, marriages would stand a better chance. This means that they take the focus off themselves and what they want and engage in genuine, meaningful communication, which includes actively listening rather than preparing a response while the other person is talking, especially when that response is fueled with an arsenal of anger, bitterness, and blame.

I will stop here because this is me talking now and not Bea, and this book is called *Some of That Bea Wisdom*. However, I did say that I might include some wisdom that I have gained along life's way. Well, if I did not, I plan to. So, as Bea said, "If you can take it, you can make it!" I live by this. It causes me to be more patient and understanding. I compromise more. That does not mean that I cop out or cave in. It just means that I acknowledge that I am not always right and that because someone does not do things exactly as I want them to, does not make it wrong, just different.

# On Relationships

*"If you don't like my peaches, don't shake my tree."*

This statement has been as gold for me. Bea would tell me that if someone, especially the opposite sex, was going to like you, they would. If not, do not worry about it. She would say not to worry, "there would always be another bus". Bea said that if a boy/man did not find me to his liking, I should just tell him if he didn't like my peaches, he didn't have to shake my tree. This taught me at an early age that just because someone does not like me; it is not because there is necessarily anything wrong with me. It might just be that the person is at the wrong tree. He wants oranges, and I am not an orange tree nor can I ever be an orange tree.

So, I have never been the kind of person who tries to fit into a mold or try to reshape myself to conform to someone else's expectations that may be unrealistic for me. That does not mean I do not look at myself critically to make needed changes; it means simply that I do not take a person's dislike or non-acceptance of me to mean that there is something wrong or deficient in me. Rather, I think first that it could possibly be that I am not what this person wants or needs. Despite the cross-pollination and genetic modification that is being practiced in agriculture today, you still cannot get oranges from a peach tree.

# On Self-Esteem

*"Why wouldn't he like you? You're smart, nice looking. You dress nice. You've got your own car..."*

What an awesome morale boost, and this was long before the movie *The Help* was released! In that movie, the star, in order to bolster the esteem of a little girl who was not pretty and was unwanted and neglected by her mother, often had the child repeat the phrase, "You is smart. You is kind. You is important."

I credit Bea with my healthy self-esteem. She knew the importance of words. She was not a psychologist or a psychiatrist but she knew that we were watching her, and when children are young, sometimes they think that the mother knows everything. She is their teacher. She is their world. So, Bea taught me early on how to respect myself and to think highly of myself and everyone around me. That included her and my father, whether I liked everything they did or not. She said I did not have to be what someone else said I was. Remember, I was one of 15 children. My father was the only breadwinner. I did not have the best clothing. I could not keep up with the styles. I did not have money to participate in many of the extracurricular and after-school activities. Sometimes I was rejected and called names, but my foundation was secure. My mother had built me up. In my mind, I knew that once I was able to get certain things and do certain things for myself, I would be fine. Thanks to her words that always spoke life to me, I never internalized the negativity. I was able to separate what people said about me from who I really was.

Words are seeds, and every seed reproduces after its own kind. I always say if you do not like what you're getting from life, check what you are saying. The words that we speak go down into the heart. So we must be careful what we plant because the harvest is going to come one day. Thanks to the loving words of affirmation from my mother, spoken again and again at an early age, I grew up healthy, happy, and reasonably well-adjusted.

# On Race

*Never forget that you are "Black"—light-skinned or dark-skinned makes no difference. To White people, we are all just Black. You just be proud of who you are!"*

Growing up, I had never experienced overt racism from Caucasians or other races; only the intraracism or colorism, racism that occurred, and continues to occur, within one's own race. As I said earlier, I did not always fit in and was not a part of any clique. So, sometimes I was picked on and called names. One of those names was "black." This was said in an attempt to hurt my feelings, and it did but not because I felt bad about being black. I felt bad because I could not understand why someone who looked like me found black to be bad.

This form of racism is harsher and more offensive than traditional racism because there is a common denominator of skin color. Although it is present in many races, it seems that the level of racism among Black people surpasses that of nearly all other races. This racism is very evident in individuals from grade school, sports figures and movie stars (especially), to individuals who are enjoying retirement. It is true that we are all African American or Black but, unfortunately, that is where our commonality ends. I am saddened and embarrassed to admit that within my own race there was and continues to be separation that is based on the shade of blackness of one's skin. It is hard for me to accept that with all the advancements we have made as Black people, we have not moved beyond the issue of skin color. Without turning this discussion into an exposé on racism, I will explain briefly.

Intraracism or colorism is a result of slavery. According to historians, light-skinned slaves were children of the slave master; they were, therefore, sometimes treated a little better than were individuals whose skin was a bit darker. Also, light-skinned slaves were more apt to work in the slave owner's house as opposed to darker skinned slaves who were required to work in the fields and were beaten more frequently. In time, light skin began to be associated with privilege; it also began to be associated with beauty according to Marita Golden, author of *Don't Play in the Sun: One Woman's Journey Through the Color Complex*."

It is sad that not much has changed. The slave master did his job well. Statistics show that most Black men prefer light-skinned females over dark-skinned ones, not because that's their own personal choice but rather because they have been conditioned and taught to choose, even to desire light-skinned or White females. Some studies show that our children have also been affected. In a recent study, pictures of Caucasians and African Americans (light- and dark skinned) were shown to children, and they were asked to choose the persons whom they thought were smartest or prettiest. More often than not, the children chose the pictures of White or the light-skinned people to represent the smartest or prettiest.

This is why I love and appreciate my mother's wisdom. She knew what we would face when we left home and she prepared us for it. One of my favorite places to shop was Garfinckel's. She told us how she was not allowed to try on hats there. Garfinckel's was a prominent department store chain based in Washington, DC that catered to a wealthy clientele. The owners filed for Chapter 11 bankruptcy in June 1990 and ceased operations that year, probably because they wouldn't allow my mother to try on their hats!

She told us about racism and how to deal with it. Then, she taught us to appreciate the beautiful skin color that

God had given us. She told us that we did not make ourselves but God did and that He was all wise, and He knew exactly what He was doing. Bea would have us use brown paint to color our dolls, paintings, greeting cards, and statues. We all helped. We thought it was great fun. It was automatic. If we bought Christmas cards or greeting cards of any kind, we used our brown crayon to color any people who were not of color. We were not allowed to make any distinctions around skin shade. My mother told us that no matter our hue, we were Black people and that we should be proud of it. So today, I am okay with my dark complexion because Bea taught me early in life that I didn't choose it but that the all-wise, loving God, Creator of the universe made me the way I am. When I hear people engage in dialogue about being light- or dark-skinned, it makes me sad that so many individuals have been and continue to be negatively affected by this kind of within-group racism. As a dark-skinned woman, I am so grateful for the way my mother "enlightened my darkness" at an early age. I only wish more of my people had a Bea in their life to teach them that they are beautiful, whatever shade they are and that one is not better than the other, just different. We used to sing a song when I was little that we would do well to teach to our children today. The lyrics were: "Jesus loves the little children, all the children of the world; red and yellow, black and white, all are precious in His sight. Jesus loves the little children of the world."

# On Being Content

*"You don't know what people did to get what they have or what they have to do to keep it."*

My mother valued being satisfied with what you had. I was satisfied during my early childhood. However, I experienced growing discontentment during my teenage years as it became apparent to me what I did not have.

Adolescence is a difficult time both for teenagers and their parents as the child transitions from childhood to young adulthood. Like most teenagers, I wanted to break away from my parents and discover who I really was, what I wanted to do with myself, and how to relate to individuals of the opposite sex. If this were not enough, I was faced with dissatisfaction about my economic circumstances. The girls in my class at school got their hair done regularly, went to parties, and some even had a boyfriend. They seemed to have everything going for them. It was not until I was much older that I understood Bea's words.

I became friends with a lovely couple. Their home was enviable because it was beautifully furnished. They wore expensive clothes and jewelry and often hosted elaborate parties. I thought the world of them and visited them often. I was impressed and would often mention them to my mother, telling her about their fancy home and parties. On one occasion, when I told her about something they had bought, I expressed that I wished that I could do the same. Bea stopped me in my tracks. She told me not to be so carried away with what people had. That's when she said, "You don't know what people did to get what they have or what they have to do to keep it." Boy, was she right! One day, I came home from work to find people hauling everything out of their home and putting tags on each piece. I later found out that my neighbors had been accused of being involved in some illegal activities and had been arrested and taken to jail. I never saw or heard of them after that.

# On Men

*"A chicken ain't nothing but a bird."*

It was my mother's view that just as a chicken is a bird, a man is a man, no matter what race, color, or creed, or whether he was a man of faith or not. It was her view that there are certain traits that exist in every man, no matter who he is, because "a chicken is a bird." What she was suggesting was that all men want sex. When I was growing up, there was not a lot of open discussion about sex. My mother would say things like when you meet a man "keep your legs closed"; there was no further explanation. When I started dating, she told me not to think that any man I met was that much different from my brothers. I had six brothers. So, I had good opportunity to confirm her statement. I was also fortunate to have been married twice to two wonderful men (not at the same time), both deceased (also, not at the same time). I was married for most of my adult life.

Once I was not married and again had the opportunity to meet and be in the company of more single men, it became abundantly clear to me that all of the men I met wanted sex; women seem to want commitment. Another observation I have made is that if a man can spend his entire time having satisfying noncommittal sex, remaining free to do whatever else he wants to do, he will do so. In this world of short-term pleasures and sexual relationships, nobody wants to "catch feelings." Most men want the sex without the strings. My finding: a chicken ain't nothing but a bird.

# On Courtship

*"Just bring me the one you're going to marry."*

Needless to say, any mother who had six teenage boys and six teenage girls in the house at the same time would at some time or another face challenges, especially around dating. One of the challenges my mother faced was that some of my brothers brought their "girlfriends" (I use this term loosely) to meet her. Bea would greet them cordially and chat with them. Sometime later, they would bring someone else. She would do the same—greet them and engage in conversation. After a few rounds of this, one day one of my brothers brought a young lady in. He left her in the living room and came back into the kitchen where my mother and I were. He said, "Bea, I have somebody I want you to meet." My mother very calmly and quietly responded," That's alright; just bring me the one you're going to marry."

I laughed so hard that I almost cried. I had to cover my mouth with my hands to keep the young lady from hearing my hysterical outburst. Bea was not being mean. She just did not want to take the time to get involved with a whole lot of young ladies in whom my brother had no serious interest. After all, my mother valued relationships, and they take time and energy. She did not want to risk investing a lot of time and energy and possibly becoming attached to someone who was not going to be around.

# *On Respect for Home*

*"This is not a house by the side of the road."*

My mother taught us to have respect for where we lived. She saw everyone who came in and out. When I lived at home, I did not have a key, and I did not think that was unusual. As far back as I can remember, my mother was always at home. When she did go out, she went with my father, and we all stayed home together until they returned.

As I grew older, it was the same. Even after some of us became young adults and were living at home, we could not come and go as we pleased. My mother still insisted that we keep "respectable" hours. My mother was wise. When some of us started dating, she knew that meant she would need eyes in the back of her head to make sure that no shenanigans took place. After all, our home was "not a house by the side of the road."

# On Taking Personal Responsibility

*"Every tub must stand on its own bottom."*

This is what Bea would say whenever we tried to blame someone else for our actions. She said we should take responsibility for our actions. Sometimes when we got in trouble for something we had done, we pointed our finger at someone else, either to blame them totally or to incriminate them somehow. She said no one forced you to do what you did. You have a mind of your own, and you should use it. Bea taught us there are certain things no one else can do for you. You have to do for yourself. Then, when you have done it, whatever it is, take responsibility for your actions because at the end of the day, every tub must stand on its own bottom.

# On Gratitude

*"Go get me an "Epsi pay- ola kay."*

This is my humble attempt to write the words Pepsi Cola in "pig Latin." Yes, that's what I said, pig Latin. This is a language game in which English words are altered. The objective is to conceal the meaning of the words from individuals who are not familiar with the rules. It is a twist of English for people who want to be silly, or for parents who do not want their children to know what they're talking about. Briefly, pig Latin requires the speaker to move the first letter of the word to the end and add *ay*. For example, *python* becomes *ython-pay*.

The church that I attended as a young girl was located next door to our house in Northeast Washington, DC, and it housed a vending machine that contained only sodas. It was always full of those little small glass bottles that contained no more than about 10 ounces of various sodas. My mother only drank Pepsi Cola. Some of you might not have a point of reference for this, but when you have 12 children in the house and you get anything sweet, the odds are slim to none that you will be able to enjoy in peace whatever it is you have. So, whenever my mother wanted to enjoy anything in peace, it had to be done clandestinely.

I was one of the few of my siblings who understood pig Latin. Therefore, I was the one most often commissioned to go and fulfill this awesome responsibility. She would call me aside and in a very hushed tone say, "Go get me an "Epsi pa ola kay." Obediently, I would run next door and discharge my duty. For some reason, without her having to explain it to me, I understood my mother's need and tried as best I could to go and get what she asked for without letting my siblings know what was going on.

Getting the soda was the easy part. The big problem was getting it back to my mother without everybody knowing she had it, and that was mission impossible because we were always around our mother. It's a small wonder we did not suffocate her. But Bea had the proverbial patience of Job; she was always cool, calm, and collected. The moment that tiny bottle of Pepsi was in her hands, we swarmed like bees. We would dash to the kitchen and make a beeline back to our mother, each of us holding our little melamine cup. Because there were so many children in our family, we rarely used glassware.

Imagine if you can kids numbering more than a regulation basketball team, all screaming in high-pitched voices, "Give me some!" What did Bea do? Like a lion tamer, she grabbed a nearby chair and beat us back with a whip! No, not really. I think that is what I would have done. However, that was not Bea's reaction at all. She had us all line up and told us to come and get our "sip." Yes, just one sip! And one by one, into each cup she poured a sip from her tiny bottle of soda. And we received it as if it were gold. We drank what amounted to not more than a tablespoon of our mother's cold, sweet nectar, and we were thankful. No one complained. No one said it was not enough, although to be sure, we would have liked it if we could have had more.

Bea always told us that when anybody gave us anything, just take it and say thank you. She said that just being thankful would open the possibility of receiving more. Bea said the more grateful we are when we get good things, the more good things we will receive. In some cases, she said, these good things will start coming more rapidly than before. Gratitude means thankfulness, counting your blessings, noticing simple pleasures, and acknowledging everything that you receive. It means learning to live your life as if everything were a miracle, and being aware on a continuous basis of how much you've been given. Gratitude shifts your focus from what your life lacks to the abundance that is already present. I thank my mother for using a small bottle of *Epsi pa ola kay* to teach me to be grateful, and I award her posthumously the Medal of Honor!

# On Help That Helps

*"I'm not going to take all your work from you."*

Many of you might have read the story of the caterpillar and the butterfly. There have been many renditions of the story. Here is one of those renditions.

Once, a little boy was playing outdoors and found a fascinating caterpillar. He carefully picked it up and took it home to show his mother. He asked his mother if he could keep it, and she said he could if he promised to take good care of it. The little boy got a large jar from his mother and put plants in the jar so the caterpillar would have something to eat; he also put a stick in the jar so it would have something to climb on. Every day he watched the caterpillar and brought it new plants to eat. One day, the caterpillar climbed up the stick and started acting strangely.

The boy worriedly called his mother who came and understood that the caterpillar was creating a cocoon. The mother explained to the boy how the caterpillar was going to go through a metamorphosis to become a butterfly. The little boy was so happy to hear about the changes his caterpillar would go through. He watched every day, waiting for the butterfly to emerge. Then, finally it happened: a small hole appeared in the cocoon and the butterfly started to struggle to come out. As the story goes, at first the boy was excited, but soon he became concerned. The butterfly was struggling so hard to get out! It appeared that it could not break free of the cocoon. It looked desperate. It did not seem to be making any progress at all. So, he decided to help. He ran to get scissors, and then walked back (because he had learned not to run with scissors in his hands). He snipped the cocoon to make the hole bigger and out came the butterfly!

As the butterfly emerged, the boy was surprised. It had a swollen body and small, shriveled wings. He continued to watch the butterfly, expecting that at any moment, the wings would dry out, enlarge, and expand to support the swollen body. He thought that, in time, the body would shrink and the butterfly's wings would expand. But neither of these things happened. Instead, the butterfly spent the rest of its life crawling around with a swollen body and shriveled wings. It never was able to fly. He learned that the butterfly was SUPPOSED to struggle. In fact, the butterfly's struggle had a purpose. In pushing its way through the tiny opening of the cocoon, the fluid would be pushed out of its body and into its wings. Without the struggle, the butterfly would never, ever fly. Instead of helping, as he thought he was doing, the boy's good intentions hurt the butterfly.

Bea never told me this story, and I do not know if she ever even heard it. But she certainly could have written a story of her own. She knew what real help was. She knew that in order to really help us, we needed to gain strength through struggle. Bea insisted that we pick up our children on time. I can remember asking her if I could pick my son up after I went shopping, or to the grocery store, or participate in some other activity. Her reply was, "I'm not going to take all your work from you." She would tell me that she had been with my child and others all day. "Now," she said, "come on and pick up your son and do anything else you want to do." Bea explained that she had worked hard all day, reading to them, teaching them their ABCs, how to count, and letting them watch "Sesame Street." Now, she said, it was my turn.

I must admit, that did not always make me happy but I can say now that it was good for me. I would never have known all that I was capable of doing if she had done that for me. I learned and my son benefited too. Because I had to take Ashanté with me to a variety of places, I had to teach him how to behave in different settings as well as how to interact with other people. This would not have been possible if Bea had allowed me to leave him with her. Sure, it would have been easier and more convenient for me not to have to deal with a young child as I shopped or did various tasks but in the end, Ashanté and I developed a stronger relationship. Not only that, but having to actually do all of the hard work that was involved with having my son made me more appreciative of what my mother was doing for me. It also made me think long and hard about whether or not I would have another child. I can assure you, though, that my mother could have cared less what I thought. She knew that she was doing the right thing. She knew that not overextending herself would not be good for her or for me. In addition, if you showed any sign of disappointment, Bea had no problem letting you know where to get off! She would say, "That's your child. I didn't get one night's enjoyment out of having him." Bea was something! I have lived long enough to see her point.

For example, I met a young lady who had a child, and her mother started out "helping" by babysitting the grandchild anytime for anything because she felt sorry for the child's parents. The grandmother wanted the parents to be able to do everything they wanted to do, or she felt that the parents were not doing enough for the child. So, she had to step in. Pretty soon what the grandmother started out doing to help became the expectation. Over time, the roles were reversed. The grandmother became the parent. The more she did, the more she had to do. Then, the daughter had another child (mom enabled her to do it. . . .). Before the mom knew what hit her, she was raising kids again. She could not go and come as she pleased. She hardly had time to do anything for herself. She had to negotiate with the children's mother to keep her own children so that she (the grandmother) could attend to her own needs.

What the grandmother did was not helping. Instead, it was taking all the responsibility away from the mother, the one who should have had it. Whenever someone tells me about a situation like this, I give them Some of That Bea Wisdom. I tell them what Bea told me and how it helped me. I tell them that I am a stronger, more responsible person today because Bea had the wisdom, the strength, and the foresight to say to me, "I'm not going to take all your work from you."

Today, I abide by the same principle. I help people but I know when to cut it off. We should know how to give the kind of help that makes people better and makes them do better. The true measure of help is whether it is making the person we are attempting to help better and causing them to do better or is it allowing them to bypass the growth that comes from struggling to do for oneself.

# On Finances

*"It's not what you make, it's what you do with it."*

As I told you early on, I was one of 15 children born to my late parents. My dad was the only one who worked. Every two weeks when he got paid, he would bring the money home to my mother. I do not know when or how it was decided which one of them would handle the finances, but Bea did. She was the chief of finances for the Robertson household. In retrospect, it could have had something to do with my father's occasional visits to the place my mother called the "beer garden." However, knowing my mother and her wise ways, she probably convinced my father, without ever mentioning it, that she would be better able to handle the finances. As for the beer garden, I did not have a clue. In my child's mind, though, I imagined a beautiful garden, resplendent with beautiful flowers, trees, shrubbery, and bistro tables—a lovely parklike setting.

I could always tell when Diddy had been to the infamous beer garden. He would arrive home a little later than usual, sometimes a bit tipsy and not himself. I did not like seeing him like that and early on developed a dislike for alcohol. I promised myself I would never become a drinker, and I have kept that promise. Nonetheless, I must tell you that having grown up and having gained more understanding, I can appreciate why my father took a drink every now and then! When he arrived home, he would go to my mother, who had usually by this time retired to her bedroom. If it was payday, he would pull out a large wad of cash and begin counting it out to her. Bea was usually seated. My father would start tossing bills into her lap, all the while muttering, "Bea, they got me again." That meant he did not have all the money he should have had.

The sight was rather comical to me but probably not to Bea. Nonetheless, at those times, she remained calm. She never engaged him in these moments. She picked up the money and put it away. Then, she went about doing whatever she was doing. I can only guess what was on her mind. She paid all the bills then allocated what was left for whatever else our large family needed. We always lived in a house, never an apartment. We always had food to eat, clothes to wear (not always what we wanted), and shoes on our feet. No doubt there was a great deal of creative financing going on, especially during times like this. Thank God this was not an everyday occurrence! I never heard Bea complain. She worked with what she had and kept everything going. I still marvel at that. Yes, I had everything I needed but very rarely anything I wanted.

When I got my first job, I thought I was rich. I bought most of what I wanted. I shopped incessantly and charged large sums on credit cards. I shopped at expensive stores and bought things I could not afford. I got heavily in debt and I had more outgo than income. Bea would tell me, "Child, if you don't stay out those stores, you won't have bloomers to put on your hind parts." How right she was. It was not long before I was in serious financial trouble.

When I grew a little older, got married, and had my son, I began to realize how expensive everything was. My husband and I were both working, and we only had one child. At that time, we lived in a two-bedroom apartment, not a house. I began to ask questions. Once I recall asking Bea how in the world she was able accomplish all she did on one salary. She said simply, "It's not how much you make, it's what you do with it." That stuck with me. I did not make significant changes right away. Actually, it took years, but it is never too late to get straight. Over time, I changed my attitude about money and spending. One of the best things I did was to curb my use of credit cards. I began to watch what I did with my money, and I never spent all that I had, and I did not waste money or spend frivolously; if I could not afford it, I did not buy it. Because of what I saw my mother accomplish in our large family on one salary, I knew that I had to do better. My father was not a millionaire. He was employed as a truck driver for the DC government. Surely, it is not how much you make but what you do with it. Now, it is important to me how I handle my money.

Someone once said that money is a tool, a test, and a testimony. Because money is a tool, we should not chase after it, hoard it, or serve it. Instead, we should use it. We must realize that it comes from God. He gave it to us to use, and we should use it as He directs. We should make sure we use some of it to help others. As a test, we should check to see how we are spending what we have. For example, when we review our bank statements, how many payments do we see for charitable giving versus purchases for ourselves. Money can be a testimony as your tax accountant prepares your returns and takes note of how much you give to advance the kingdom of God.

# On Making a Difference

*"Brighten up the corner where you are."*

Bea always said that you cannot fix everything, and you cannot help everybody. You cannot do everything but everybody can do something. So, do not try to save the world, just brighten up the corner where you are. In other words, do what you can where you can with what you have. I am grateful for her words because this world is so full of pain, adversity, and suffering that it can be overwhelming. It is easy to become cynical and stoic and to think that there is nothing that can be done. But because of my mother's advice, when I see or hear of people in dire circumstances or come upon troubling situations, my first thought is, what I can do to help, how I can ameliorate the circumstances? I just want to do whatever I can to help. I realize that what might seem little to some might mean the world to someone else. So, when I see someone hurting, I ask God, "what can I do?" When I see people in need, I ask, "what can I do?" When I see death and destruction all around, I am not overwhelmed by the enormity of the problem. I just try to brighten up the corner where I am.

# On Dealing with Difficult People

*"Handle them with a long-handled spoon."*

This is a nugget that I have shared with many people and one that has been so beneficial to me. When people have a disagreement, whether with family members or friends, many tend to want to end the relationship altogether. That's like throwing out the proverbial baby with the bath water. However, Bea taught me to handle difficult people with a long-handled spoon. In other words, keep a healthy distance; take them in small doses. Don't give up on the relationship simply because it's challenging. She taught me to analyze the value of relationships. Some people might be a little hard to deal with, but they might also have skills and abilities that could be useful to you. That relationship might be worth developing. Others may not be worth the time. Time is our most precious, treasured commodity. We can make money but we cannot make time no matter how much money we have. Also, none of us knows how much time we have. Therefore, unless something valuable is at stake, we should not waste time trying to deal with someone who insists on being difficult.

Bea taught me that some people in our lives, whether family, friend, or co-worker, are just not worth the hassle. She said that we should love them, help them when they need it (if you can); otherwise, handle them with long-handled spoon because your time is too valuable. Unless there is something important at stake, do not waste time on people with whom a relationship will only add stress and undue pressure to your life. Deal with this kind of person on an as-needed basis. In so doing, you can make the most of every relationship.

# On "Premature" Death

*"If they die while they're young, they won't have this race to run."*

It was years before I came to understand the wisdom of this statement. When I was young, it was rare or at least unusual to hear of the death of a child. I recall one such instance when I was about 8 years old. Bea told us that a young girl was missing and feared dead, and we all were terrified. We stayed really close to her all that day. She could not walk without us at her feet, terrified at the thought that someone close to our age could suffer such a fate! Nowadays, such occurrences are more frequent, making people less sensitive to such a tragedy.

I am not totally sure what triggered Bea's response. Perhaps it was the seemingly senseless, premature death of her two innocent babies. Often, when a very young person dies, there is much talk about what that child might have accomplished had he or she lived. But Bea had a different outlook. She did not think about what that child could have achieved but rather what they might have been spared from. She said, if they die when they are young, they do not have this race to run. How profoundly true! We do not often hear this at funerals or home-going services. As I said, most of the talk and the sadness is about what could have been. But my mother was a wise woman. She was able to see things from God's perspective. Again, when Bea shared information with me or made statements, she did not always say that this is what the Bible says. However, after I began to read and study the Bible for myself, I found these words written by the prophet Isaiah in 57:1—"Good people pass away; the godly often die before their time. But no one seems to care or wonder why. No one seems to understand that God is protecting them from the evil to come." As Bea used to say, you could have bought me for a penny! A light bulb went off.

My mother understood that God is really in control, that He knows what He is doing! So, while some people might have seen the passing of my dearly beloved son Ashanté and others I loved as premature, I did not think that way. In the midst of my grief and sorrow, I could see God at work. Now, more cases of violence against our children result in death. I take comfort in the Bea Wisdom that came from God: "If they die while they're young, they won't have this race to run."

# On Thinking Before You Act

*"Use your head for something
else besides a hat rack!*

Before the United Negro College Fund ever adopted as its slogan, "A mind is a terrible thing to waste. . .", there was Bea! Whenever I or one of my siblings said or did something that made no practical sense (more times than I care to recall), Bea would admonish us to use our head, not as simply a place to wear our hat but to remember that in our head a brain was housed and that we should use it to think. She told us to always think before we spoke because words once spoken could never be retrieved. She also taught us to think before we took any action because our actions have consequences. She said that you could not just bump around life unthinking because there were people out there who did not love us and who, she said,

65

were thinking while we were asleep. She wanted us to be vigilant, thoughtful, and wise. I can still hear her voice of wisdom, "Use your head for something else besides a hat rack."

# Summary and Conclusion

*Wisdom is the principal thing; Therefore get wisdom. And in all your getting, get understanding.*

*Exalt her, and she will promote you; She will bring you honor, when you embrace her.*

*She will place on your head an ornament of grace; A crown of glory she will deliver to you.."*

*Proverbs 4:7-9 NKJV*

What I have shared here are kernels from the storehouse of wisdom my mother shared with me over her lifetime. There are many others that I cannot quote readily but that pop into my brain just when I need them most. One thing about wisdom is that it is timeless. It does not go out of style. The words my mother shared with me decades ago are just as relevant and valuable today as they were then.

Hardly a day goes by that I do not thank God for Bea. I am still living by the wisdom she imparted to me, and I am sharing it with others. I have become more grateful that she was a praying mother who sought the wisdom of God for her family, and she shared Some of That Bea Wisdom with me. I pray daily that God will endow me with wisdom like the Wisdom of Solomon for my own life and for everyone who comes into my sphere of influence. I agree wholeheartedly with the word in Proverbs 4:7—"Getting wisdom is the wisest thing you can do! And whatever else you do, develop good judgment."